Testimonials

Harry,

I wanted to take a moment to express my gratitude and appreciation for your hard work in managing this process. I'm sure that your coaching and advice have played a key role in my being selected for the position as Chief Operating Officer. Not only the coaching you have given me but also for your advice to me. This is a great opportunity and without your help and hard work it would not have ended so positively for me. So, I am in your gratitude and look forward to a continued business relationship in the future. Thank You!

Warm Regards,
KP

Dear Harry,

I wanted to thank you for your interviewing preparation last week. I had felt that my credit skills were a bit rusty, which is why I did not appear that confident when I initially met you. However, your graciousness, and generosity helped me feel much better. I thought you had some great ideas and I valued your polished approach and interviewing techniques. I believe my interview with the bank went well, and I owe it all to you. Thank you again, and I will be happy to refer my colleagues to your company.

Gratefully yours,
BD

Hi Harry,

I think the interview coaching gave me a realistic big-picture of what an interview really is. Thus minor things that one would overlook in individual preparation, such as the hand shake, eye contact, seating position, etc. were addressed and the "right" way to do them was discussed. Essentially, what I think is important, and did not realize before, is that these might be minor details, but what if the interviewer is one who focuses on these types of details?? You might as well be prepared because the bottom line is you can blow it simply because of a minor detail.

I think personally I needed the most work on body language, which before the coaching I had never realized. In preparing for these interviews I would be so caught up on technical details that I never really gave thought to the manner I was speaking in or the way I was seated. The coaching put a spotlight on an aspect of the interview I had previously completely overlooked. "Act in a solicitous manner" was the single phrase which probably made the most difference to me. Before the preparation I had been to a couple of interviews, but in trying to show confidence I realized later I had instead been condescending and even arrogant. I think being solicitous during an interview shows the interviewer two crucial aspects which I am sure they look for: *1*. that you are excited about the prospect and *2*. that the prospect peaks your interest.

The interview preparation also helped me structure my thoughts and stories in a way which was easy to convey. Sometimes when explaining things, particularly job responsibilities, if you are not prepared and particularly clear, it is easy to confuse the other person or interviewer. Simply the thought process of writing out different work related stories helped me organize and prepare them in my mind. Thus on the interview I was sure the interviewer was understanding my job responsibilities clearly and not just nodding and going on to the next question.

Many thanks and best regards,
H D

Harry,

I wanted to thank you again for the interview prep work that you covered with me on Tuesday morning. I did a good amount of homework that night, and felt very confident, prepared, and relaxed going into the interview at GS. The interview went very well, and GS has asked me back to the 2nd round for a position that is more senior and aligned with the work that I would like to do. Thanks for all the great pointers, I truly believe that our talk made a difference in the outcome of my interview.

Regards,
R.J.

INTERVIEWING:

It's Your Big Deal

by HARRY DRUM

Bloomington, IN Milton Keynes, UK

authorHOUSE™

AuthorHouse™
1663 Liberty Drive, Suite 200
Bloomington, IN 47403
www.authorhouse.com
Phone: 1-800-839-8640

AuthorHouse™ UK Ltd.
500 Avebury Boulevard
Central Milton Keynes, MK9 2BE
www.authorhouse.co.uk
Phone: 08001974150

First published by AuthorHouse 8/28/2006

ISBN: 1-4259-4674-7 (sc)

Library of Congress Control Number: 2006906164

Printed in the United States of America
Bloomington, Indiana

This book is printed on acid-free paper.

<u>Dedication</u>

To my wonderful and supportive wife Cindy who encouraged me to write this book.

To my three wonderful children of whom I am so proud– William, Cara and Jonathan who all critiqued and added their two cents.

Especially William, who I now realize is a caring adult who took the time to edit this book slowly and conscientiously, careful not to bruise my ego.

And to my brother Brian who gave me the opportunity to learn how to be an interviewing coach.

CONTENTS

I. INTRODUCTION

This is a how-to book on interviewing.

It is for the person who is qualified to do the job. It is also for the person who wants to maximize their opportunities to get the best job offer. There are qualified people who do not interview well. The book is a common sense approach to an important process which leads to a major life event – getting a job.

The information presented in this book is based on tested personal and professional life experiences, as well as hundreds of successful interviews and coaching experiences. It has aided candidates in getting good jobs for all levels of jobs from administrators to CEOs. Three times in my life, I have been hired to be the president or general manager of different companies. Each time I was coached on interviewing. Each time I was offered the job! Eight years ago, I joined an executive search firm where a level of coaching was given to senior candidates. Using that experience, I developed this new process and have used it to help many executives significantly improve their interviewing skills.

For the past eight years I have been helping others to learn how to interview effectively. In addition to utilizing this approach in helping qualified candidates prepare for interviews I have given classes at career centers at some of the top universities in the country. The topic of the class: how students can best prepare for that all-important life event, interviewing and getting the first "real" job.

The process has evolved over several years. It has been revised at least five times by me in the past five years. When you are through with this book… And you believe in the process, you will be asked to perform a self-analysis exercise which I call the *Homework Assignment*. It should take you three to five hours. You might even want to read the book more than once. Certainly, you should dust the book off and review it every time before you go on a job interview. I recommend refreshing your interviewing skills at least 48 hours before the event. Reading the book and doing the homework may take five hours. It may take longer. Take as much time as you need to prepare.

Ultimately, reading the book – and doing the preparation diligently, (- don't wait until the night before the interview) should give you the confidence that you will perform well. If you have most of the skills to do the job and the chemistry is right, this process usually puts you "ahead of the pack" and will help to get you the best job offer.

Most of us spend years preparing for weddings, months preparing for childbirth, and even a day preparing for a funeral. But most people think we can go into a job interview without any real preparation. Simply, this is because a person thinks that if he/she can do a job, he can get it. These are two different skills; *doing the job* and *getting the job*. This book is about the developing the skills needed to get the job. It assumes that you have the skills to do the job!

This book is neither a guarantee of success, nor a foolproof way to get a job. It is not about tricks! It is a five hour, workbook approach which guides you on how best to prepare for a job interview.

II. WHY SHOULD YOU PREPARE FOR AN INTERVIEW?

Let us assume that you are applying for job with a base salary of $100,000. The company pays you benefits which are not readily seen in the base salary but usually cost the firm up to 35% of your base pay. (Social Security expenses and unemployment insurance expense alone cost the employer about 13 %.) In addition you might get a bonus of 20% of the base salary as an added incentive. Total cost to the company is now approaching $160,000.

Additionally the company provides you an office. Let us say that it's 80 square feet. This might cost the company annually, an additional $2400 at $30 per square foot for the space you occupy. Add this to your phone costs, computer, furniture and disposables, like paper and energy and the company has spent another $5,000 per year driving your total hard dollar cost thus far to about $165,000 for the year. Companies hire you, to add to their bottom line; to create or improve the profitability of their company. Every employee directly or indirectly must help the company make income; otherwise the company would be a charitable institution! Even charitable institutions need employees who will enhance their productivity.

Each employee is typically expected to contribute 10 times their cost to the bottom line income of the company. Obviously some don't, so each new person is expected to bring in that amount to make up for the losers! (One might say that the best company has the least amount of losers.) We call this opportunity cost. The $100,000 base executive, who really costs $165,000, has another $1,650,000 in annual opportunity costs associated with his employment. This is the biggest risk a manager can usually take in a firm, hiring a new executive.

Add these elements together, and the company is investing about $1.8 million annually in the candidate; both with the hard cost of paying for you in the year and the opportunity cost associated with the risk of hiring you.

For a $100,000 annual base paid executive in a typical company the real cost is closer to $2 million - and this is just for the first year of employment. Most people expect to stay on the job for several years and get salary increases... If we assume an expected tenure on the job of five years, with annual raises, the total cost to the company, both in hard dollars and opportunity cost, of hiring the $100,000 executive is closer to $10,000,000 {5 X $1,650,000 plus the salary increases and their multiples.}

If you were making an investment of $10 million, wouldn't you want to do more than just kick the tires? Sure you would.

Not every manager or interviewer consciously realizes that hiring the right person is a huge financial responsibility. This fact is good for the candidate. Think of the "awesome weight" on the interviewer's shoulders, if he understood that he was making a $10 million decision. Candidates would never get hired! But subconsciously, managers know that they are making an important contribution in the hiring process; he or she just may never have determined the magnitude of the task in quite these terms.

Getting a job is a big deal. The candidate should realize this as well. Understanding the magnitude of the transaction is a first step in managing the interviewing process to one's own benefit.

The typical executive works and commutes between 45 and 80 hours per week. Next to sleeping which takes up 30% of a person's hours, work can occupy as much as 47% of available waking hours. Besides using up most of your alert hours, an individual earns money on the job to pay for the home including food and all the other things which occupy the 23% of time where you can do what you like (which includes doing laundry, eating and other family and sundry activities.) Relatively speaking, for most of us, the job is more important to our total life situation than the $10 million for five years is to the employer, as shown in the last segment. The proportion of your time spent preparing for the interview, and the benefits that job provides for the individual, make the interview one of the most important events in one's life. It should be right up there in your priorities with marriage, kids, choice of home, and funeral and the other events for which we prepare so long and hard!

III. THE BASIC CONCEPT

I usually start the interviewing coaching process with a few open-ended typical interviewing questions. My purpose is to get a baseline of the candidate's interviewing skills.

It is important that a candidate has the skills to do the job. I always try to ascertain that the candidate does have the requisite skills, although it is not always easy. As a search firm, our role was to find candidates with the right skills. This book assumes that the reader has those skills.

One uses the skills to get a job only a few times in a lifetime.

<u>The skills to get a job are very different than the skills to do a job.</u>

Try to answer the following questions with no preparation:

Why are you qualified to do this job?

What are your strengths?

What are your weaknesses?

What sort of compensation are you looking for?

If you could design the ideal job for yourself, what would it be?

In response to the above questions, I find that most candidates respond with uninteresting and common answers. More often than not the candidate repeats the same thing that is on their resume.

Preparation for a job interview is important.

You should be prepared to spend three to four hours doing the

Homework Assignment

Get into a positive mood.

Spending a few hours preparing for a job interview, can be one of the best investments that you can make towards your future career and income potential. Spending this time will be among the best investments that you can make towards your future income and happiness. A three and a half hour preparation process, before an interview, can yield 10 to 15% more in starting salary.

Additionally, all future increases that you receive build off of that base as you work your way up the corporate ladder in that company. So in fact, if you get a higher starting salary your future income can grow exponentially! The preparation helps you get the job you want which should also make you happier!

Have you ever sold anything?

Understanding the basic concepts of **selling** is imperative to the interviewing process. I often ask candidates if they have ever sold anything. Some say "yes", and some say "no". I ask the candidate to draw an upside down "V" the on a blank piece of paper. This upside down "V" represents two legs of a stick figure. A stick figure, being that little "line man" that we usually drew when we played hang-man as a child. The legs are the base, the foundation of the sale.

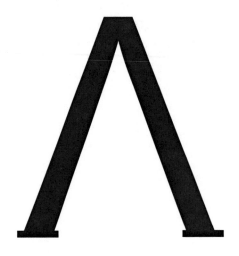

What are the two most important factors that a salesperson should be concerned about when he or she makes a sale?

Think of a "new house" salesperson. When it is time to sell that new home, the salesperson knows all about the house. He/she may know the type of construction, materials, windows, heating units, and siding from which the house is made as well as the neighborhood and site elevation, and tax rates. He or she may also know about the area schools and community organizations and a myriad of other details or "benefits" of that house. The salesperson would also know the price and the value of the house and how it compares to other builders and other competition as well as a host of other facts.

The salesperson always knows the **benefits of the product**. Every good salesperson that does his job well understands and can explain the **benefits of the product** which he is selling.

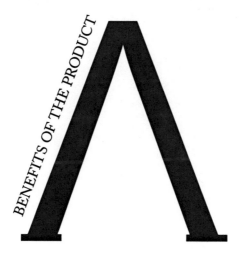

That is half of any sales transaction. The other half of that "V" has to do with the customer... A good salesperson must understand the **needs of the buyer.** Simply, if a salesperson can match the **benefits of the product** with the **needs of the buyer,** this will typically, result in a sale. In the case of the house buyer, the salesperson would want to know about the buyer's needs: number of bedrooms needed, size of family, type of house preference, garage size, budget, and credit worthiness if there are mortgages involved.

The "needs of the buyer" are the other leg.

If the salesperson shows the right house with all the amenities, the **benefits** that the buyer is looking for, thus meeting all of buyer's **needs,** the salesperson will make a sale.

*Think of a young child on a hot summer's day selling lemonade in front of his apartment house in Forest Hills, New York City. It's 100° outside. Now consider Joe, an exhausted commuter. Joe has gotten on the subway and is headed home. He's off to Forest Hills, Queens from his job in lower Manhattan. The subway breaks down for one full hour. It is very hot. It is like an oven in that subway. Finally the train gets moving again. Joe gets off at his stop in Forest Hills Queens. He is drenched with sweat; he's hot and he's thirsty. He walks a few blocks to his apartment and he sees his next-door neighbor's kid selling ice cold lemonade for $.50 a glass. He immediately lays down a dollar. He quickly drinks two glasses of lemonade and he is refreshed. The **benefits of the product**, cold and wet, **meet the needs of the buyer,** hot and thirsty. A sale is made. Simply, the **benefits of the product** met the **needs of the buyer**, so the young child made a sale.*

In another situation, *think of a group of cardiac surgeons. They regularly perform open heart surgery. They are approached by a salesperson from the medical technical division of the Hewlett Packard Company which has developed a special type of equipment with a cost of five hundred thousand dollars. The salesman explains that through extensive clinical trials, the machine can help the physicians perform three- open heart surgeries per day. They normally can do only one. The fee for open heart surgery is about $50,000. If the doctors use this machine they not only conduct three surgeries instead of one daily, making $150, 000 per day, but they are not as tired at the end of the day. It is also apparent from the clinical studies that the quality of the surgery is better and the recovery time is faster for the patient. The doctors evaluate the salesperson's presentation and they buy the machine. Here again, the* **benefits of the product** *met the* **needs of the buyer,** *and the salesperson made a sale.*

Whether selling a fifty cent glass of lemonade or a $500,000 piece of technical equipment, when the "benefits of the product" are matched with the "needs of the buyer," the salesperson can make a sale.

Why is an interview like a sale?

Because an interview is a sale!

An employer is looking for an employee to fill his or her _needs_ of performing certain tasks or duties. The employer is willing to pay sums of money to the person selected to do these tasks. The employer has a _need_: to get the job done. The potential employee has _benefits_, his or her skills and abilities to do the job.

What is the product in the interview, which is called a sale?

The product is you, the candidate, and your skills!

Who is the salesperson in the sale?

The salesperson is you, the candidate!

The key point here is that **interviewing is selling**. You, the candidate, are both the salesperson and the product.

It is no matter what your work experience has been: whatever you have been doing for the last few years; whether you have been a credit analyst or shopkeeper or a banker or candlestick maker. You probably have not perceived yourself as a salesperson.

But now you realize, in the sale we call an interview

You are the salesperson!

You are also the product!

There are two sets of skills those businesspeople (or anybody who's working) need to survive and progress in the world of work today. Most important is the skill set that you need *to do the job*. This book assumes that you have the skill. The goal in this book is to give you a method to prepare, so that you have those other, not too often used skills; the skills *to get the job.*

This is what this book is all about; learning the skills to get the job. I believe that it is unethical to tell you what to say. I won't tell you that. Interviews are highly personal and subjective events. Under no circumstances, am I suggesting that you do not tell the truth on an interview. Nor do I want you to fabricate any pieces of your background. Throughout this process I will give you a "skeleton" to build your interview. It will be your job to put the "meat on the bones".

One of the key concepts here is preparation. Most candidates do not prepare for an interview. Most people that do prepare often prepare the wrong things. Just by investing a few hours in focused preparation, you will be way ahead of the game in the interviewing process!

We will go through many aspects of the interview, but let's start with the basics.

The presentation of this book is more in the normal order of a typical good interview. I will tend to go over details as they come up in the course of the interview to make the logic flow more normal. There are parts of the interview that are more important than others. This book is not presented in priority order but in the order of good interview "flow." In discussing the process, I will be providing you with many nuances of interviewing, as well as some of the key skills that I believe help the candidate perform best on the interview. Many of the points I suggest may seem trivial or unimportant. It is often the overlooked aspects that impact the decision to hire a person. The "detail" should not be overlooked.

Several times throughout the process I will recap what we have learned. The recap technique is based on years of interviewing and successful candidate coaching experiences. This is a very pragmatic approach to preparing for an interview.

The first concept that you have learned at this point and something that will be a common theme throughout this process: **interviewing is selling.** The theme is repeated often throughout.

To make a sale you have to match the benefits of the product with the needs of the buyer. You must never forget that an interview is a sale. Your role in the process is both that of the **salesperson** and that of the **product.** It is important to know your dual role in this sale called an "interview."

The rest of this book is a step by step process guiding you how to prepare for the all important interview. Each chapter guides you through the process. I call it the "homework assignment."

At the end of the book, there are workbook pages which are "fill-in-the-blank." All of assignments you should prepare are explained in detail, first in the book. After reading the book, you should attempt the assignment at the end.

Feel free to look back into the text of the book for a more detailed explanation of how to prepare.

IV. THE HOMEWORK ASSIGNMENT-
EXPLAINED

Interviewees commonly and often make reference, early on in the interview, to their resume or CV (curriculum vitae). The candidate will very often use the expression, *"as it says on my résumé"*....or *"I have seven years experience..."* If you think about that phrase for a moment, you realize that you are suggesting that the interviewer has not read your résumé. This is a very subtle form of an insult to the interviewer.

Your objective at the end of the interview is ultimately to get a job offer. At the very least, you would like the opportunity for a second interview, to get closer to the job offer. Although you haven't meant to, you have insulted the interviewer.

If you want somebody to give you something, even a second interview, I don't believe it's a good idea to insult them!

Another common expression used by interviewees is when the candidate refers to the employer's job requirements. Often the candidate will say,

"Based on what you are looking for, I have all of the experience that you require to do this job".

Here again we have another pitfall for the interviewee. He or she has subtly insulted the interviewer. One would hope that the interviewer knows what he or she is looking for!

It is the interviewer's job to evaluate if the candidate has the skills and abilities to do the job. When you flatly state to the interviewer that you have all the qualifications that he or she is looking for, you are in fact insulting them by doing their job. Why continue on the interview at all? Let the interviewer do his or her job. That job is determining if you have the skills and suitability to do the job. Your opinion here is just not warranted.

In summary, do not insult the interviewer. Don't say *"As it says on my resume"* or, *"I have all of the qualifications that you are looking for;"* or words to that effect. If the former statement were correct, why were you there at the interview? Why didn't you just report for work that day and start collecting a paycheck?

Avoid any subtle insults to the interviewer.

Earlier I said that you should **not** refer to your resume during the interview. It is probably best not to mention your resume at all. After all, your resume is a marketing document. It did its job. It got you in the door for the in-person interview. The role of the resume is to get the candidate the in-person interview. And once you are there, the resume has done its work for you.

Since you don't have your resume to refer to; what tools do you have to make the sale?

All you have at the interview are **words** and **body language.**

The nuances of impressions and body language will be discussed later on in this text. At this point, we are going to concentrate on the words.

Have you ever seen a child's dollhouse? I like the concept of a child's dollhouse because when you look at an open-ended dollhouse, you can see all of the rooms at one time. For the next part of this process I would like you to perceive your brain as kind of an open-ended dollhouse that we can look into. Let's not call it a dollhouse though. Some people might be offended by that connotation; let's call it a warehouse.

In the warehouse I want you to segment your experiences and your vocabulary into different rooms. Most people reading this book, are being hired for their cerebral abilities; their brains! You'll prepare words and thoughts in rooms in your warehouse, so you can retrieve them when needed for the sale.

The only way that an interviewer is going to know what's in your brain is by the words that you use. That's why I believe that words are so important. Often people think that they can see into your brain through your eyes, the eyes being the window to the brain. I also believe that. I will talk about eyes and eye-to-eye contact later, when we get into the discussion on body language.

A. Warehouse of Words and Experiences

As part of your preparation process we will segment your warehouse into five different rooms.

1. Education

2. Strengths and weaknesses

3. Esoteric skills

4. Generic business skills

5. Personal chemistry

WAREHOUSE OF WORDS

Room #1: Education

The first room that I want you to go into, is the **education room.**

Depending upon where you are in your career education plays an important role. You might have a four-year degree, (bachelor's degree,) a master's degree, a doctorate degree, a law degree or no degree at all.

During the course of your work experience you may have been asked to take a course, perhaps just a few days, perhaps one that lasted six months, which helped you upgrade your skills for your job.

The task here is a meaningful one. Often if your formal education was several years ago, an interviewer might not ask you anything about it. In the perfect interview, in my opinion, education is usually covered on the resume and may or may not come up in the interview. I believe that 97% of the interview will be about other things, other experiences particularly those related to work. But if education does come up, you should be prepared!

The interview preparation necessary for the education room is simple.

Assignment 1:

Create three sentences that connect a course of study or an educational experience to the job for which you are being interviewed.

Assignment 2:

Questions the interviewer might ask could be like the following:

How has your education impacted your career?

What subject courses have you taken in either your bachelor's or master's degrees which have helped you the most in your career?

Tell me what you have learned in school.

Prepare three concise responses which connect your education to inquiries like the above.

An example of these might be;

I learned many things in my formal education; however the most important thing that I learned was in my management 101 class where I learned about the importance of participative management. In every position I have had, I have used the principles of participative management to gather input from the people who are actually doing the work and I integrate their hands-on experience into my decision-making as a manager before changing their work routines....

Another example:

My very first course in creative writing taught me to think like the "reader". I have learned to reread everything I write from the perspective of the reader. This has helped me to communicate effectively in memos to all people that I've worked for as well as people who work for me.......

Another example:

My undergraduate work was in the area of molecular biology and chemistry. When I realized that I didn't want to be a physician, I joined the work force and wanted to be successful in business. I understood early on, that I did not have good knowledge of reading financial statements, so I took a course in managerial accounting which gave me key insights into understanding the important numbers in business, particularly sales and expenses.....

Another example:

I recently took a course with the Association of National Advertisers, on how to communicate effectively with both creative types and account types at advertising agencies. It really opened my eyes to the importance of the impression that I give to "creative types" when criticizing their work. Sometimes, "agency creatives" work very hard to develop their ideas. One word of criticism not expressed thoughtfully can crush that person's ego. My role as brand manager was to get the best copy out of the agency. Roughshod criticism was not going to accomplish that.......

The above examples are just a few samples of how you should construct your three sentences about your education. Of course, you want to understand the job that you are applying for and find elements of your education that support your candidacy for the job that you are being considered for.

If you are a candidate who does not have a formal education you should not be intimidated by this question. Instead you should be prepared. The advice that I give a candidate who has no formal education is number one, <u>be prepared with an answer for this type of question.</u> Often a qualified candidate has years of experience. In my opinion, experience "trumps" education. This is not the case with everyone. Interviewers take the safe road, hiring a person with a degree because it is defensible to his superior. This fits into the old cliché that nobody ever made a mistake purchasing business machines if they bought IBM.

Clearly, education opens doors for entry-level candidates. Those candidates that have achieved success levels without a formal education have a wonderful answer to the education question, and it should emphasize their experience.

Listed below are typical questions which may be asked of the candidate without a formal education.

"Why is it that you did not get a degree?"

Or

"I see that you have no formal education. Can you tell me about that?"

A prepared candidate might answer this way:

"All of the firms that I have worked for have required a degree. Obviously I don't have one, I had to work twice as hard and learn twice as much to get to the level that I have achieved.".......

There is no guarantee that the above response is going to get you an opportunity where the firm has very strict educational requirements. I have seen many senior executives without degrees in firms that require them. They have gotten over the hump of no degree by using similar responses. Again the key here is to anticipate the question and to be prepared with a quality response. And remember, your resume has already done its job. It has gotten you in the door for your in-person interview.

WAREHOUSE OF WORDS

Room #2: Strengths and weaknesses

Two favorite questions in interviews relate to strengths and weaknesses. The questions about strengths come in several forms. The interviewer might say, *"What are you good at?"* Or *what do you do well?* Or, *what are your strengths?*

The most common and the most boring answer I hear to these questions are:

I am people oriented.

I am very organized.

I'm very detail oriented.

I am a very analytical person.

I get the job done.

The common theme here is that these answers have **no substance**. A peek into the future of this text will advise you to never talk about a skill that you have without backing it up with some proof, but we will discuss that further on.

At this point of preparation, we are just collecting words in your warehouse. We are building this interview from the ground up. In stressful situations i.e. (a job interview) it is difficult to remember, without preparation and recent review, all of the professional and relevant skills that you have.

Much of what I am teaching you here is **to prepare**. I strongly suggest that you prepare for the interview at least twenty-four hours before the event. Rest, and then review it again the night before. Sleep on it. The concept here is that much of what you should say should be prepared but still fresh in your mind the day of the interview. By preparing in a quiet place where you have time to review your myriad of experiences and years of education, the most relevant data about you will be **recent and top of mind** during the interview.

What Is a Strength?

A strength, when asked about on an interview, meets the following three criteria:

    I.   Job related

    II. Something you do well

    III. Something you like to do

Delve into your most recent work or educational experiences and pick out five skills that you have, that meet the above three criteria. When you have those five skills listed, you will have a list of your best job related skills or strengths. The interviewer should only be interested in your job related strengths. Here again, (and we have a little foreshadowing of what is to come later), I want you to think of experiences where you have utilized those strengths.

Once you have completed this task, if anybody asks you what your strengths are, they will be ready for you in the forefront of your mind. Developing this list of strengths will help you answer a multitude of popular questions that come up on interviews about what you do well.

We are still just collecting words and thoughts in room number two of your warehouse.

I have not told you how to put them together, although you might be getting some clues at this point.

Weaknesses

The "weakness question" is among the most dreaded questions asked of any interviewee.

What are your weaknesses?

Everybody hates this question. It is human nature to avoid disclosing personal weaknesses. But the real reason everybody should hate this question is because it's the "disqualifying" question. The interviewer is really asking you; *"Tell me the reason why I shouldn't hire you"*.

Here you should remember one of the key points in interviewing.

<u>Interviewing is selling</u>

When was the last time that a salesman told you about the weaknesses of his product?

Salespeople don't tell you about the weaknesses of their product.

Let's go to an example of the couple buying a brand-new SUV. The salesman points out all of the great qualities about the car. Its color, its weight, its horsepower its roominess etc. when asked about the mileage, he tells you, "If you go for this type of luxury car, why would you be worried about the mileage?"

It is believed that 95% of qualified candidates do not get job offers after interviews. Personally, I think that many candidates disqualify themselves in the "weakness" response.

That is an astounding statistic. Take the example where an employer interviews five people for one job.

He or she will only be hiring one.

In that example alone, 80% of the people will **not** get the job. If the employer doesn't hire anyone out of the five, 100% of the candidates did not get the job. The averages, as stated earlier are that 95% of qualified candidates do not get job offers. The odds are against you before you walk in the door! The key to reversing that is to be prepared!

It is not your job, nor is it in your best interest, to give the interviewer any reason to disqualify you. Any interviewer can disqualify any candidate at any time for any reason, because interviews are highly subjective. Remember, salespeople do <u>not</u> talk about the weaknesses of their products. That doesn't get them orders! The "order" to the interviewee is the "job offer." Do not tell the interviewer your weaknesses.

So how you handle the weakness question?

The definition of a weakness for purposes of the job interview **is a lack of knowledge ... in the past.**

The interviewer may pose the weakness question in many different ways: Be prepared to recognize the question!

What are your weaknesses?

Where do you fall short?

What are you not good at?

What's your weak suit?

All the above questions are the same. Be prepared to answer the weakness question, no matter how it is disguised, no matter how many times it is asked or no matter in what form the interviewer is asking it.

You may tell the interviewer about something you did not know how to do in the past, but something you have since learned.

We will talk further about how to handle the weakness question towards the end of the book. Right now you are just collecting words in the strengths and weaknesses room of your warehouse. In thinking about your weakness, *that being a lack of knowledge in the past,* I will give you an example of what I mean.

Let's pretend that one year ago you did not know how to work the common software program, Microsoft Excel. During the course of the past six months you have learned Microsoft Excel. You are now neither an expert, nor do you use it too often, but you do know how to work Microsoft Excel. When you did not know how to work it, it was a weakness. It is no longer a "weakness", though it may not yet be a strength.

Most candidates who go on a job interview believe that they can do the job. In reality, most candidates don't believe that they have weaknesses in their area of expertise.

In particular when interviewing for professional positions, I counsel candidates that they usually earn more income and have more education than 99.9% of the world's population. This makes them close to perfect when it comes to material standards (salary and benefits), job and educational achievements. Most are professionals. I ask these professionals a simple question: *"When your most recent boss pointed out your failings (weaknesses). Did you fix them?"* The answer is usually, yes. I then tell them, I guess you have fixed your weaknesses.

When you did something wrong the first time, did you realize it was the wrong way? Probably not! If you did you would not have done it that way. What makes you a top tier professional is your ability to do tasks correctly the first time. You usually don't make the same mistake twice.

We are still just collecting words and experiences. It is easy for you to leap ahead and see where we are going with this.

**A weakness is a lack of knowledge......
in the past.**

WAREHOUSE OF WORDS

Room # 3: Skills Inventory/Esoteric Vocabulary

The most important concept, after the basic premise of 'preparation' for the interview, is to review one's skills and esoteric vocabulary. This is the most significant part of candidate refreshment during the preparation process for the interview.

Candidates are often asked the question;

Why are you qualified for this job?

They usually respond that they have multiple years of experience and they are familiar with the qualifications necessary to do the job. Some add their educational background and degrees into this answer.

Example:

Q: *Why are you qualified for this job?*

A: *I have seven years of experience and a Bachelors Degree in Accounting and I have all of the other qualifications you are looking for.*

In this instance the candidate has given the hiring manager no new or interesting information about his or her qualifications. This is data which was probably on the resume. There is so much information that a candidate can provide to a hiring manager that will enhance his or her candidacy. Why waste time referring to information that they already have? You were most likely brought in for the interview because this information was already gleaned from the resume.

The notion of **<u>Esoteric Vocabulary</u>** is the major concept here.

For example, think of accountants. They deal with numbers, income statements, balance sheets, cash flow statements, debits, credits, aging reports, accounts receivable, accounts payable etc; I could go on and on. These words (and the knowledge behind them) perhaps are boring to the accountants or the controller. Yet these are the words and concepts that qualify that candidate for the job.

The interview is the opportunity for the candidate to show (to sell!) his or her competencies for the position for which he is being considered. Most people are hired for their 'cerebral' ability and their knowledge of the field in which they are working. Hiring managers want to know if the candidate being interviewed can do the job. Logically, knowledge of the necessary vocabulary and expressions that are used on a daily basis in the job or in the previous assignments of the candidate, are what qualifies him or her for the position.

The process here is for the prospective candidate to create a list of vocabulary words which are unique, "esoteric," to the profession. The candidate should put himself in a mindset where he is explaining the duties and the responsibilities of his or her job to a twelve year old. If the twelve year old does not know the word, it is good enough to put on your list!

Yes it is that simple. *The interviewer does not know what you know! Don't assume that he or she does.*

Assignment

The candidate should develop **50 vocabulary words or phrases** which are specific to the position for which being interviewed. It is not necessary to write down definitions of all of these words. The interviewer's assumption is that if the candidate knows the word he or she knows its definition. This exercise helps the candidate to refresh himself with the general skills that he has to do the job.

Refreshing yourself with words or expressions which are used commonly in your current job and probably in the job that you are being interviewed for will help you identify skills and depth of knowledge in your field of expertise.

After completing this part of the preparation you'll start feeling more confident in your ability to talk about your skills. The concept here is one of refreshment, taking inventory of your skills so you can recall them the next day during the interview.

By reviewing the vocabulary of one's trade, the candidate confirms a firm grasp of the tools and the skills necessary to do the job. An interviewer will be impressed with your basic and advanced knowledge of the skills needed to do the job by your correct usage of esoteric vocabulary.

70% of the interview should surround your discussion of your esoteric skills and vocabulary; this is absolutely the most important part of your preparation.

WAREHOUSE OF WORDS

Room #4: Generic Business Skills

Are you organized?

Do you manage your time well?

Do you know how to work Microsoft Excel?

Have you ever supervised anyone?

Most candidates are able to answer yes to the above questions. As a seasoned business person, you probably have developed many business skills. The skills mentioned above, like organization, time management, software skills, and supervisory skills are considered generic skills. In addition to your esoteric skills you probably have a variety of generic business skills.

Listed below are 30 generic business skills. You may be able to do all of them well. When you are interviewed for a position, it is usually assumed that you have both esoteric and generic business skills. In most cases the esoteric skills are more important in the hiring decision. That is not to say, that generic skills are not important. If the candidate were to tell the entire story of his or her work experiences and skills he or she could probably talk for a few weeks!

Interviewing is selling. You as the candidate have 45 to 60 minutes to make a "very important sale". Most of your words on the interview should work for you. Don't waste your time or the interviewer's time, talking about skills which are not relevant to qualifying you for the position at hand. Don't assume that because something was obvious to you, perhaps as stated on your resume, that it is just as clear to the interviewer.

Listed below are 30 generic business skills. Some of them may overlap your esoteric skills. For example, a general manager may have supervisory and managerial accounting skills. These skills are important to his ability to do the job and may constitute a high priority with the hiring manager. In some cases these skills may be more important then his knowledge of the particular products that the firm may be selling.

Assignment

From the list below select a <u>dozen</u> generic business skills that you feel you perform well. These strong generic skills are in addition to the 50 esoteric vocabulary words or expressions selected in the previous section. Select the generic skills which you believe are most relevant to the job for which you are being considered. Add your own if I have left any out.

List Out of Generic Business Skills

Verbal communication skills
Marketing
Learning
Educational/work related studies
Evocations/hobbies/Athletics/other interests
Written communication skills
Management potential
Supervisory skills
Decisiveness
Project management
Time management
Organization
Planning
Operational
Administrative
Financial
Analytical
Quantitative
Qualitative
Follow-through
Creativity
Computer literacy
Programming
Computer hardware
Consultative
Mentoring
People handling
Political
Selling

WAREHOUSE OF WORDS

Room#5: Personal Chemistry

At this point in the process you will have collected four rooms of vocabulary and experiences tied to four categories; educational background, strengths and past weaknesses, esoteric vocabulary and skills, and generic business skills. You can have the best of all of these words in your vocabulary and it will still not get you the job as there is another important factor that employers look for before making a hiring decision. This relates to your potential 'fit' into the company. In addition to your personal demeanor and your body language (which comes later in the book) the only way that a potential employer will know if you fit, is by the words that you use. You have to speak the company's language!

Like all of the four categories before, there are words that describe your personality and personal chemistry. I call these words chemistry words. This section should be as important to you as it is to the Company you are working for. If you don't fit in you will be uncomfortable, leading to unhappiness on the job. Getting a job is a serious event. You will spend more time on the job, if you are typical employee, then you will with your spouse, your children, or anybody else that you have loved or cared for. Many believe that personal chemistry or 'fit" is the most important consideration in getting a job. Happiness on the job is important. Good chemistry is a major factor in making that happen.

It is thus important that through your vocabulary, that you give an accurate picture of the type of person that you are, and how well you will fit into the organization.

Assignment

Select a dozen words from the list below which describe your personal chemistry. Pick out words that portray you. The list below could be 1000 words long and certainly all the words that describe your chemistry are not included. The list below is just a sample of many words that describe a person's chemistry. Use them as a guide to determining twelve that best describe you. Pick words that you feel would be important to your ability to do the job.

After you have selected these words, run them by someone who knows you very well to see if he or she agrees with your perception. You might say, *"I am going on an interview tomorrow and I'm going to use these 12 words to describe my personality."* Say them slowly. If your friend who knows you well, chuckles, at any one of the words, choose another! If you can't convince a person familiar with your life that these are words that describe you, you won't be able to convince a stranger!

Why only 12?

Here again the time factor comes in to play. During an interview you will have 45 minutes, perhaps an hour to make a major sale. You have to pick the words that work the hardest and best for you.

Sample List of Chemistry Words

Use these or other words which best describe your business personality or chemistry.

Hard-working
Strong work ethic
Discipline
Leadership
Tenacious
Responsible
Industrious
Determined
Motivated
Decisive
Personal
Easy to get along with
Outgoing/extroverted
Careful
Shy/introverted
Timely
Eager to learn

B. The Vignette

You are done collecting words.

At this point in the process you will have five rooms filled with words and experiences and categorized in the areas of **education, strengths and weaknesses, esoteric skills, generic skills,** and **personal chemistry.** Now, how do you put all this together?

In your current assignment or job do you solve a problem a day?

It doesn't have to be a big one. For example you might have corrected the words in a memo that went out under your boss's signature. You may have proofread the document and effected a change that provided clarity to its meaning. Or, you may have solved a problem that helped save your company $500,000.

Most people answer the above question with a simple answer; that they solve multiple problems per day.

An executive who has worked for five years and solved a problem a day has solved five problems per week, 250 problems per year and 1250 problems in five years. If the person has solved two problems per day, with the same math that turns into solving 2500 problems in five years.

Wow!

That's a lot of problems!

Every job is really about solving problems.

A new employer will hire you if you can prove to them that you know how to solve the types of problems they anticipate they will have on-the-job they are interviewing you for. The best thing that you can share on an interview is your ability to solve problems. I suggest that you do that with a <u>simple proof</u>. The proof or evidence is true stories about your career where you have solved problems. You can adapt the following formula to your years of "problem solving" in the workplace. Figure out the number of small and large problems that you have solved for your recent and past employers.

Assignment

While looking over your resume and thinking about your most recent and former jobs, make a list of 25 problems that you have solved in your career. Each problem should have a two or three word title. It is not necessary to write out each problem in prose. It is important that you say each problem out loud verbally, at least the night before the interview. Convert each of these 25 problems into a short story, a vignette, explained henceforth.

The structure of each vignette should be prearranged in the following format:

$$V=P+S+B$$

V   is for **<u>vignette</u>**, a short story about your career.

P   is for **<u>problem</u>**: after you have given a clear concise background statement about the firm you work or worked for; **<u>then clearly state the problem.</u>**

S   is for **<u>solution:</u>** once you have identified the problem, very conversationally discuss the solution that you or your team came up with to solve the problem.

B   is for a **<u>benefit</u>**: imbedded within the solution there should be an obvious benefit to the firm that you work or worked for.

Utilizing many of the words you have collected in your warehouse, and using your resume as a guide, tell true stories (vignettes) in the above format, (P+S+B) about the problems you have solved in your different jobs.

Companies hire us to bring them a benefit. If you can provide solid examples of how you have brought benefits to the firms that have employed you, a new employer will believe that you can bring similar benefits to them.

C. Understanding Your Benefits

Why create 25 vignettes from your career?

You will probably only have the opportunity to tell five or six benefit stories. Good salespeople have inventory. Your vignettes are your inventory; true stories about your career where you have identified and solved problems to the benefit of the firms that you have worked for.

Of course, when telling your vignettes you should incorporate the vocabulary which you have collected in the five rooms of your warehouse discussed previously.

Fill your vignettes with esoteric and generic vocabulary, strengths, and personal chemistry. Refer to educational background only when it is a necessary part of the vignette.

When you have completed your 25 vignettes, you will have the <u>benefits of the product.</u>

The tenet of this process is to remember that interviewing is selling. Remember that at this interview:

<u>You the candidate</u>

<u>are both the salesperson and the product.</u>

To make a sale the salesperson has:

<u>to match the benefits of the product</u>

<u>with the needs of the buyer</u>.

Your benefits are your vignettes!

We are more than halfway there!

When we started this exercise we talked about an interview being a sale.

To refresh, we said that there are two legs to a sale.

One of those legs, <u>understands the benefits of the product.</u>

You now understand that this interview is a sale; and that you are the <u>product.</u>

The benefit of the product (you) is your history and experiences.

<u>The best benefit that you can give a new employer is proof that you can do the job.</u>

Your vignettes are your proof;

those 25 short stories

including

<u>a problem, solution and benefit.</u>

A true story about you!

D. Understanding the Employer's Needs.

The next part of this process, in this interview, that we call a sale is to understand the **needs of the buyer.** A good salesperson always understands the needs of the buyer before he or she goes in to make the sale.

The best way for a candidate to understand the needs of the buyer, the prospective employer, is to have a complete and full understanding of the job description. The candidate should also know something about the hiring company. This can be gleaned by reviewing the company's web site, and or by reviewing annual reports or other industry literature in the public domain about the company. In today's internet age, the best way to get this information is from the web: "Google" the company! However if you do not have access to the Internet you should use your local public library and or your recruiter.

Understanding the company is 5% of your preparation process in regards to understanding the needs of the buyer. It's great to be informed, but don't over do it!

The most important thing you can do is to understand the job description.

First; I want you to read the job description five times, so in fact you have a very good handle on what this job is all about. At this point I would like you to disregard the years of experience and educational levels that the employer is looking for in the qualifications section of the job description. The most important areas that you should look for in the job description are the <u>duties</u> and the <u>responsibilities</u> of the job.

Once you have "digested" the job description, create a list, in **<u>bullet point format</u>**, which itemizes in priority order the listed duties and responsibilities of the job for which you are being interviewed. You might be surprised that it takes a couple of tries to do this.

The title of this list should be:

Duties and Responsibilities.

Below the title, you should create between five to seven bullet points.

Once you have this list you will have the **<u>needs of the buyer</u>**.

You now have both legs of the sale called an interview; the needs of the buyer and the benefits of the product.

The needs of the buyer are the bullet points which you have created from the job description

The benefits of the product are the 25 vignettes or short stories you previously created which highlight your ability to identify and solve problems to bring benefits to the firms for which you have worked.

In the next set of pages I have given you a sample job description for a brand manager in a consumer-products company.

On the next page after careful review of the job description I have created seven bullet points which are the key duties and responsibilities of this job.

You should do the same with the job description of the position for which you are being interviewed.

Sample of a Job Description

Job Description

Title: Product Manager

Reports to: Category Directory

Responsibilities: The product manager in the chewing gum category will work to increase the market share of the assigned brand. Included in the overall responsibility will be the charge to increase revenue, maintain/decrease expenses and profitability of the product line. This position also provides direction to sales, promotion, packaging, distribution marketing research and advertising. The brand manager will also have responsibility to train and develop an assistant brand manager and marketing assistant.

Duties:

1. Forecast the brand sales on a monthly/yearly basis.

2. Ensure that packaging is current and meets all government and regulatory requirements.

3. Evaluate and create cost effective advertising strategy for the brand in conjunction with the advertising agency.

4. Recommend market research projects that provide information to improve the product vs. itself and its competition.

5. Develop sales strategies and plans to increase Nielsen/ Market share.

6. Coordinate materials for the sales department to sell the product to the trade in conjunction with other company products.

7. Develop promotional packaging and events to further improve brand awareness and distribution.

8. Create promotional trade programs and calendar for the brand coordinated with other company brands.

9. Work with research and development to create new formulas to improve product vs. competition.

10. Keep management and other relevant departments informed of all issues regarding the brand.

11. Train and develop assistant brand manager and marketing assistant.

<u>Requirements:</u>

<u>Educational:</u>

BA/BS Degree – MBA preferred

<u>Work:</u> 5-7 years experience with a major consumer products goods company

- Duties and Responsibilities

- Run the day to day operations of the brand including forecasting sales.

- Create programs in conjunction with the advertising agency which increase sales for the brand.

- Create programs with sales and promotion departments to increase sales of the brand

- Decrease expenses associated with the brand to improve profitability

- Create new line extensions for the brand with R&D

- Train and develop key subordinates

- Keep senior management informed

Your goal during the interview is to match your benefits (your 25 vignettes) to their needs (those 5-8 bullet points.)

You will not have the opportunity to tell anybody 25 stories in an interview.

So why prepare 25?

Simple.

A good salesperson has lots of inventory. Your vignettes are your inventory.

E. Matching

At this point in the process I want you to focus on your bullet pointed list of needs of the buyer; those five to seven statements which you have defined in priority order as the needs of the buyer created from the job description.

You should carefully reprioritize your vignettes, so they match the priorities which you have created in your bullet pointed list of their needs. You should make sure that you have at least two vignettes to match each one of the bullet points.

Your goal during the interview is to tell five to six vignettes that match, **in priority order,** the five to six bullet points created from the job description.

In a very conversational manner, you will be telling them five to six true stories, vignettes about yourself. You will use words that "speak their language." You will prove that you can handle the most important duties and responsibilities of the job for which you are being interviewed.

This is the essence of this process.

You understand that interviewing is selling.

In order to effectively make a sale you have to match the benefits of the product with the needs of the buyer.

The benefits of your product, in this interview are your vignettes which you have prepared and said aloud the night before.

The needs of the buyer are the five to six bullet points that you have prioritized from the job description.

You now have a framework of the interview. Your goal is to tell them six vignettes that prove that you can do the job.

As the interviewee, you know what you want to accomplish during the interview. You want to tell them six to seven good stories that match their needs, which you have gleaned from the job description. Those proofs will qualify you for the job. That is your plan for the interview.

Unfortunately, the interviewer asks all the questions.

However many questions are asked, there is only one question that a job interviewer wants answered:

Can you do the job?

I have asked this question of thousands of prospective candidates. The answer is always yes; or absolutely; or without a doubt. I have never gotten a "no!" Maybe this is why nobody ever asks this important question because it is always answered in the positive and with no doubts.

You should assume, regardless of the words used in any question by the interviewer, that every question actually is:

<u>Can you do the job?</u>

However, I do not want your answer to be just an affirmative yes.

I want your answer to be:

<u>Yes I can, and here is proof.</u>

Your proof is your vignette.

It takes some practice to get from the question to your proof. You should develop a few "segues" to your vignettes.

Most of the time, an interviewer should be more concerned with your answer then with their question. A good interviewer is happiest when they get qualifications and proof from the candidate that he or she is qualified to do the job.

Sometimes, interviewers are more nervous than the candidates they are interviewing. Most line managers spend only a tiny fraction of their time interviewing. It is not a skill many managers use often as part of their job. Logically, hiring a new person, even in a growing company, is something performed relatively few times during the year. One would hope, that hiring managers are spending the bulk of their time doing their jobs, creating income for the firm, and not interviewing. A good line manager will welcome the fact that you have given him or her enough information which qualifies you for the job.

On the following pages I have given you examples of four difficult interviewing questions and possible answers. I want you to read them carefully. Come to your own conclusions.

The candidate is being interviewed for a position as a Private Banker working for a prestigious New York firm. Joe currently works as a private banker for a similar firm.

One of the key elements of the job description requires the executive to bring new high net worth clients into the bank. Here is the verbatim transcript of the question and the answer.

Interviewer: "Joe, Tell me, what are your strengths?"

Joe responds: "I have been a private banker for the last five years. I enjoy working with high net worth people in..... And I remember a few years ago a gentleman called the office and the call was given to me. He was a rather cantankerous old guy. He actually started yelling at me. He said, "I've got $4.2 million in stocks, I'm retiring this year and I can't pay the electric bill with stock certificates; what can you do for me? I informed him that I needed to know more about him before I could answer such important questions as to managing his financial affairs. I kept him on the phone for about 45 minutes and I convinced him to send me copies of his most recent brokerage statements. (He was a doctor in Scarsdale, New York by the way.) He had his secretary overnight me copies of his most recent brokerage statements. When and I reviewed the statements the next day, I was horrified. He had over 30 different accounts. It looked as though he was hit by every 'stock jockey' in the nation. When I analyzed his portfolio, I realized that if he sold all of his securities on that day he would've had losses of over $250,000. When I apprised him of that, he almost did not believe me. I said Doc, when you consolidate all of your statements onto one document it's apparent that you have realized these losses. Of course when he saw my faxed document he accepted that. I then recommended an asset allocation program where we put 70% of his money into quality corporate bonds with two to three-year maturities. On that portion of his portfolio we were able to get about 8%. The other portion of his portfolio we put into quality growth stocks, mostly blue chips. We bought them on the market dips so we could get him some value into his portfolio. In total we were able to produce about $270,000 in annual income net of our annual fee of $25,000. His annual income needs were about $220,000. I said Doc; you'll probably live to be 100 years old, so save your pennies. In 15 years $220,000 won't buy what it'll buy today. You will need the extra principal to generate more income as the years go by. I know that this was a long answer to your question...... but I think it gives you a picture of my skills as a private banker. Have I answered your question?

If you think the above answer was too long – hold that thought. That is an important point and we will address it later in this section called "the temperature question".

First let's diagnose:

The above was a vignette. $V = P+S+B$

Identification of the problem (P):

The doctor was retiring and he needed income.

The solution(S):

We got the doctor income.

Benefits to the firm (B):

$25,000 in annual fees

$4.2 million new assets under management

Possibility of referrals from the doctor.

F. The "Temperature" Question

As stated earlier, interviews are subjective events. This process has tried to give the candidate a format to provide factual information to a prospective employer. The process is one of matching historical true stories – the candidate's benefits - with the needs of the buyer, taken from the job description.

If the candidate tells lengthy stories to an interviewer who likes to hear short, concise answers, it is unlikely that that candidate will get the job.

Conversely if they candidate gives terse answers to an interviewer who likes detailed answers, that candidate will also probably not get the job.

The same interviewer who wants detailed answers on Monday might want short concise answers on Tuesday!

This is a further complication for the candidate. How do you know which path to take?

To resolve this issue I have developed the concept known as the "temperature question." The candidate must figuratively take the temperature of the interviewer. It's about time management!

You might ask, "Do we have time for detail?" Or

"I know you are busy, would you like me to be brief?"

The candidate will usually get an answer from the interviewer like the following:

"Please, take your time; I really would like to get to know you."

In the above example, the interviewer is suggesting that you may take your time and give him more detail.

The interviewer might also respond oppositely:

"I'm really glad you asked. Unexpectedly, my boss has called me about a conference 30 minutes from now. So if you could keep it short, I would really appreciate it."

If the response to the temperature question is like the one above, you should fashion your vignettes to be briefer.

Most managers make the hiring decision in the first five minutes of the interview. (No one ever admits that, but it is clearly the case.) It is always in your best interest to tell the vignette which qualifies you to do the most important responsibility or duty of the job first.

You rarely get a second chance to make a first impression. Your answers to first questions are very important.

Be prepared. Prioritize the job responsibilities and your vignettes. Conversationally, their needs will be fulfilled by your benefits.

G. Serial Interviews

Candidates rarely get hired with just one interview. In larger corporations it is typical to be interviewed by the human resource manager, two or three line managers and a more senior line manager.

The good news here is that it is beneficial for the candidate to repeat himself. Interviews are not cumulative.

If each interview with each person, was a mirror image of the previous interview that would be good.

Each interviewer is not looking for something different. They are usually all looking for the same thing. Can you do the job?

So whether you are being interviewed by the human resource manager, or any of the line managers, feel free to repeat yourself. It is really O.K. to tell the same vignettes over and over again.

The cadre of people who have interviewed you may caucus and compare notes. One or two of the interviewers will re-tell one or more of your vignettes. One of the others will say, "She told that to me also." You will have instant credibility. This type of feedback will garner comments about you reflecting trust and credibility, components essential in the hiring decision.

Feel free to give detail to a human resource manager interviewing you, even (especially!) if the interviewer is not a technical expert. The human resource manager will appreciate learning about your area or of expertise and the vignette process lends itself to that. Don't be concerned that a human resource person does not understand the esoteric jargon of your job. Remember, each question by each interviewer is "Can you do the job?" regardless of their position in the company.

You have choices

There are many different possible answers to open-ended questions. You don't always have to give the most obvious answer to a question asked. Always take a moment, 1 ½ seconds, to think about how you are going to respond to a question.

You are signaling to the interviewer that he or she has asked an important question. Your response says, "This important question deserves a thoughtful response." Interviewers appreciate quality answers and they feel respected by this type of response.

Listed below are several questions which candidates have difficulty with. Some of them are "trap" questions. For the following three questions, I have provided the usual, common answers as well as suggested thought-out responses.

There are some additional pitfalls that we will go over.

H. Four More Difficult Questions:

1. Why are you looking for a job?

2. What compensation are you looking for?

3. What would you do if............. ?

4. What are your (really, you can tell me) weaknesses?

1. Why are you looking for a job?

Usual responses:

1. In my current company I have reached the "top of my game" and there is no future for me there.

2. There has been a change of management and I see the handwriting on the wall.

3. My company is moving to another state and I am not going to make the move.

4. My company merged with XYZ company and they have eliminated my job.

In all of the above responses the candidate has provided information irrelevant to his or her qualifications for the job. The candidate has provided information that can potentially hurt his or her chances in being made a job offer.

In responses one and two, the interviewer can conclude that your current employer understands that you are not promotable so why should he hire you?

In response number three, the interviewer can conclude that you are not a company man. "You are not willing to meet the former Company's needs, so why would you meet my company's needs?

In response number four, the interviewer can suppose that somebody is performing your function even though they have eliminated your position. Why were you the one eliminated?

<u>A better response to this question might be:</u>

I received a call from a headhunter telling me about this job and it sounded like quite an interesting opportunity. I always like more opportunity and responsibility and this position seems to offer more of both.............finish with a vignette.

Words like <u>responsibility</u> and <u>opportunity</u> are good words to use in an interview.

2. What sort of compensation are you looking for?

Usual responses:

1. I am looking for between $100,000 and $110,000.

2. I will accept the lateral move in salary because I am unhappy in my current position.

3. I would like to earn more than I'm currently earning.

4. I am not ready to discuss salary yet and I would like to learn more about the position.

In response number one, the candidate will clearly accept $100,000 because $100,000 is between 100 and 110. Why should the employer offer him more than $100,000? Why should he hire such a poor negotiator anyway?

In response to number two, the interviewer subconsciously assumes the position of the candidate's current employer. The interviewer concludes that it is the candidate's fault that he or she is unhappy. Why should I hire somebody who has made their current employer so unhappy? They will probably do the same to me.

In response to number three, the interviewer might assume that the candidate is unhappy as in number two. In any event, the employer is doing the candidate favor by improving his or her current situation. This answer does not benefit the candidate or company – it's not responsive.

In response to number four, an interview is a sale and price is a major component of a sale. Most interviewers will not ask any questions about salary on the interview; particularly the first interview. If the interviewer does ask about it, he or she is usually anxious about making a financial commitment to the candidate. Response number four just puts the interviewer off. It is likely that the interviewer knows what the candidate is currently earning either through the headhunter or in response to the candidate responding to a price in the advertisement for the job.

<u>A better answer to the salary question might be as follows:</u>

"I am certain that if I have the qualities and qualifications which you are looking for at XYZ Company, you will make me the right offer. I am not worried about that…. (Add a vignette.)"

3. What would you do if......?

When posing this question the interviewer usually has a solution already in mind. If you do not verbalize a solution in your response, close to his mindset, you probably just disqualified yourself. Logically, you are not an employee in that company yet. You do not know the people and their culture. In an interview setting, you most likely have not been given all the background to even come up with the same solution.

A better way to approach this question is with the vignette answer:

"I am sure that I couldn't possibly have all the information to solve this problem. However, I had a similar situation in *Company XYZ*, and this is how I approached it........ V= P+S+B."

In this response, you are giving an answer where you have complete control of all the variables. Your history and inventory of personal vignettes are the best pieces of evidence that you can provide on an interview.

After you have taken the "temperature" and responded well during the interview, expect to <u>again</u> get the dreaded question:

4. *Tell me, what are your weaknesses?*

Usual answers to the same question, when asked later in the interview:

You have heard these before in the strengths and weaknesses section of the text.

1. I'm a perfectionist.

2. I am too detail oriented.

3. I expect too much from my subordinates.

4. I put in too many long hours.

5. I don't spend enough time with my family.

Most interviewers like candidates who do things perfectly, who wouldn't? The same goes for candidates who are detail oriented, have high standards for their subordinates, and those who put in long hours.

I do not see how a candidate wins with any of the above responses.

When the interviewer asks this "terrible" question (again.) remember that he or she is looking for a reason to disqualify the candidate. Salespeople do not talk about the weaknesses of their products while making sales. An interview is a sale; do not talk about your product weaknesses.

So how do you get around the dreaded question? Especially, when the interview has been going so well?

After years of pondering this question I was given an answer by a relatively young candidate who I believe offered one of the best answers to this "silly" question.

The candidate was being interviewed for a position as a financial analyst with a hedge fund. He had been a financial analyst who had done extensive financial modeling for the current firm he had worked for. After doing the homework assignment, he understood that the first bullet point in the needs section created from the job description was that of financial modeling. This is how he answered the question; **tell me what your weaknesses are?**

His response verbatim:

"The last time my boss pointed out my weaknesses to me I corrected them. I remember my very first day on the job at Citigroup three years ago. My supervisor handed me a pile of spreadsheets, 17 high. The president of the division needed them completed by eight o'clock the next morning. I had not even turned on my computer yet. When I did turn it on all it had was Microsoft Excel. It did not have Lotus 1-2-3 which was the spreadsheet that I was used to using. I asked around and nobody had it. I searched out the computer geek and he gave me the tutorial and handbook for Microsoft Excel. It took me two hours to learn it; I worked till 11 o'clock that night. I was able to get all of the spreadsheet done with the income statements, balance sheets, and cash flow statements completed. I constructed them with all of the variables that the president had requested. They were on his desk at eight o'clock the next morning. When I don't know how to do something in order to do my job I consider that a weakness and I make it my business to learn it. I hope I answered your question."

Let us now diagnose his answer.

What was the problem?

The president needed the spreadsheets done.

What was the solution?

These spreadsheets were completed on time.

What was the benefit to the Company?

The president was able to make the correct decisions for the company based on the spreadsheet analysis.

The above answer given by the financial analyst to the weakness question was a classic vignette.

Some questions about our candidate above:

Does he understand income statements?

Does he understand balance sheets?

Does he understand cash flow statements?

Does he meet deadlines?

Does he put in long hours?

Is he a quick learner?

The answer is obviously yes to all of the above questions.

Our candidate skillfully talked about his ability to do the job. He answered the one question which was not asked, but the only question that the interviewer wanted to know:

Can you do the job?

What is his weakness???

He didn't offer any, like a good salesperson. He actually took the question off the table by preempting future similar questions with his segue, "the last time my boss pointed out my weaknesses I corrected them."

You must be prepared for the weakness question to be asked more than once. In fact the key to this whole process is preparation and practice.

The last page of your worksheet provides you with a list of the 17 most commonly asked questions on interviews. You should ask yourself each of these questions and see if you can respond with a segue and vignette.

I. Prepared questions

1. Don't Ask Benefit Questions.

Remember that an interview is a sale. Good salespeople don't ask questions which benefit themselves. The candidate shouldn't ask questions which seek personal gain.

Contrary to popular thought an interview is not a mutual "do we fit together" process. An interview is a sale. Until you receive the job offer (preferably in writing), it is not advised to ask any questions which benefit you the candidate. Such questions do not satisfy the prospective employer's needs.

Inappropriate questions include those about benefits, bonuses, vacations, sick leave, 401(k) plans or other benefits.

There will come a time, when the table will turn, after you get the job offer. Then you will be buying and the employer will be selling. That is the best time for you to ask questions which benefit you. At that time, you have not accepted the job, but you have been given the offer. You are the "chosen." If a headhunter is involved, it is best to let the headhunter ask the questions for you. Here is where you let the headhunter be the bad guy if need be. You may have the offer and it is not just right and it is sometimes awkward for you to negotiate for yourself. The headhunter has more experience then you do in these matters.

2. Since You Asked....

You should have one or two "big picture" questions for the interviewer if he asks a question, "Do you have any questions?"

It would be best to structure two questions that are relatively innocuous. I have had a client tell me that they liked everything about the candidate however; they could not believe that the candidate did not have any questions.

Questions like the following would be appropriate:

Can you tell me something about the structure of the department that I will be working in if I get this job?

How do you see the Company growing in the future?

Have two big picture questions prepared.

J. Body Language

Your body language is extremely important because it helps to set the "temperature" of the interview. You communicate with your body and facial expressions as well as your words. Listed below are key points that an interviewer might notice. You may want to ask yourself questions, in front of a mirror, and take note of yourself. Try to see yourself as the interviewer does. Smile! The vibes you project will be received – and often returned by the interviewer.

a. Dress

Nowadays business people are more casual in attire than ever before. That is okay for them, but absolutely not for you! You should look like an executive, from the tip of your polished shoes to your neatly and cleanly trimmed hair. Regardless of the office position you are applying for you must dress like "the banker." (Dark suit/pressed shirt or blouse/club tie, and minimal tasteful jewelry.)

b. Handshake

People judge you by your handshake. It sounds crazy, but they do. Make sure that you have a firm (but not bone breaking) handshake. Athletes (men or women) should avoid a too forceful grip. Young women (and men) should avoid the impression of uncertainty that a weak handshake can make. The crux of your hand should meet the crux of the interviewer's. (That spread between your thumb and pointer finger.) If there is some physical reason why you cannot shake hands explain it briefly. Smile and make eye contact.

c. Notes

Do not take notes. This will be clearer as to why, in the 'eye to eye' section. You may want to bring several copies of your resume with you; use black and white only. Offer one only if you see the interviewer "groping." Perhaps he or she has misplaced their copy, or Human Resources failed to provide one. Say, "I happen to have an extra copy of resume, if you need it."

d. Listen Carefully

When the interviewer is talking he/she is usually not listening to you. As soon as the interviewer speaks, that is your cue to stop what you are saying, even in the middle of a word. Don't feel that you have to finish that thought. When the interviewer starts talking it is usually a good sign for the candidate. They have probably subconsciously decided to hire you and they are selling you the opportunity. Let them talk.

e. Positioning/Posture

Sit with your back straight-up and your hands clasped in your lap. If you are more comfortable with your legs crossed, that is okay too, but not preferred. It is best to keep your feet squarely on the floor. It helps to keep you from fidgeting. Lean in to your questioner occasionally. (Move both of your shoulders and your torso slightly forward.)

f. Eye to Eye Contact

Make constant eye contact with your interviewer. You should always look directly at his/her eyes. This builds trust and credibility. This is more a cultural habit than anything else. In some cultures, e.g. Asia, it is actually rude to look at the person's eyes.

g. Smile

Smile occasionally. It is a sign of confidence. It suggests that you are pleased to be there.

h. Breathe

Practice taking a breath for one and half seconds after you are asked a question before you answer. It gives you time to think. It also suggests to the interviewer that he has asked something meaningful, and deserving of a well thought-out response.

i. Other Objects

Do not hold pens and other objects in your hands. They become toys. Objects may distract the interviewer's concentration. You want the interviewer to pay attention to what you are saying.

j. Clichés

People use all figures of speech like, "ya know", "absolutely", "exactly" and a host of others. Cliché phrases used in casual conversation have no place in the interview.

K. The Thank You Note

You should send a brief thank you note immediately to each person who has interviewed you for the job. It should be short. It can be in an email. Don't use "kitsch" or pictures – be professional.

Check the spelling carefully, especially of the interviewers' names. Be careful with the names of the company or organization. If offered a business card, accept it gratefully. On balance, however, it's best not to ask for one. It does not benefit the interviewer and could be misinterpreted.

__Thank the person for his or her time.__

__Do not get effusive.__

__Add a line of your continued interest.__

SAMPLE:

Dear Mr. Jones,

Thank you for the time you spent with me and for giving me the opportunity to learn about XYZ Company. I continue to have interest in the opportunity.

Sincerely,
Your name

V. RECAP

Interviewing is *selling*. An interview is a big ticket sale.

You, the candidate, are the *salesperson;*

You are also the *product.*

To make a sale you have to *match the benefits* of the product to the *needs of the buyer.*

Your benefits are your *vignettes:* short true stories about your career that describe how you have solved problems giving a benefit to your company or organization. Each **vignette** contains a **problem**, a **solution** and a **benefit**.

$$V=P+S+B.$$

The needs of the interviewer are buried in the job description.

Understand the needs of the buyer, the interviewer, in advance, by listing in order of priority the duties and responsibilities in bullet point format from the job description.

Prioritize your vignettes to match their needs in a very conversational manner by converting every question they ask into the all-important one: *Can you do the job?*

Your answer is *Yes I can, here is proof!*

VI. HOMEWORK ASSIGNMENT

Warehouse Room #1

<u>Educational Background</u>

Prepare three (3) sentences that **relate your education to your line of work**. Education may include any of your graduate, undergraduate courses or any relevant coursework or seminars you have participated in through your jobs.

1. _____
_____
_____ ....

2. _____
_____
_____ ....

3. _____
_____
_____ ....

Homework Assignment

Warehouse Room #2

Strengths and Weaknesses

List five (5) skills that meet the following three criteria below. These are considered your "strengths" for interviewing purposes:

    a. Job related.

    b. Something you do well.

    c. Something you enjoy doing.

1. _____

2. _____

3. _____

4. _____

5. _____

Weakness

Do salespersons talk about the weaknesses of their product? No. Do not forget that an interview is a sale.

A weakness defined here is a <u>lack of knowledge</u>.........in the past.

_____

_____

Homework Assignment

Warehouse Room #3

Skills Inventory Developmental History
<u>Esoteric/Technological/Highly job related vocabulary/</u>
<u>lingo.</u>

Make a list of fifty (50) words or expressions that are used
in day to day work that are unique to your profession and
the job you are being interviewed for. Each word will relate
to a skill that you have to do your job. It is not necessary to
put down definitions, just the words.

1. _____	15. _____
2. _____	16. _____
3. _____	17. _____
4. _____	18. _____
5. _____	19. _____
6. _____	20. _____
7. _____	21. _____
8. _____	22. _____
9. _____	23. _____
10. _____	24. _____
11. _____	25. _____
12. _____	26. _____
13. _____	27. _____
14. _____	28. _____

29. _____

30. _____

31. _____

32. _____

33. _____

34. _____

35. _____

36. _____

37. _____

38. _____

39. _____

40. _____

41. _____

42. _____

43. _____

44. _____

45. _____

46. _____

47. _____

48. _____

49. _____

50. _____

51. _____

52. _____

53. _____

54. _____

55. _____

56. _____

Homework Assignment

Warehouse Room #4

<u>Generic Business Management Skills</u>

From the list below, select and circle twelve skills that you have which are not included in your list of esoteric skills noted in Room #3 above. You may be good at all the skills listed but only choose twelve. You have limited time to talk on the interview so pick the skills noted below that are job related and where you have higher ability. Add any that are not listed but that you believe are generic and relevant.

Communications Verbal/ Written
Management
Supervisory
Delegation and Follow-up
Decisiveness
Project Management (has a beginning and an end)
Time Management
Organizational
Planning (non-functional)
Operations
Administrative (Paper flow, Record keeping, Bureaucracy)
Financial (Finance, Accounting budgets, Short term planning, Strategic planning)
Accounting (CPA requirements, Cost accounting, Managerial Accounting)
Analytical
Quantitative
Qualitative

Priority Setting

Creativity

Computer literacy (Programming, using software i.e. Microsoft Office Suite, Lotus, dBase, etc.)

Computer hardware (PCs, LANs, Network, Mainframes, etc.)

Consultative/ Advisory

People handling skills

Political skills

Selling

Marketing

Learning skills/ Quick study

Educational – work related studies

Avocations, hobbies, athletics, other interests....

Homework Assignment

Warehouse Room #5

<u>Personality/Chemistry</u>

From the list below, circle a dozen (12) words which describe your personality and chemistry. The list is a short one. Take the liberty of increasing the list to include several of the thousand words which describe personalities. Pick only 12. Here again, time is important and you cannot talk about everything. During the one hour interview they only know what you tell them. Run these words by a significant other the night before the interview. Tell that person that you are going on an interview tomorrow and you will be using these words to describe yourself. Say them slowly. If he or she laughs at any one of them pick a different one. If you cannot convince your "significant other" about your personality, you will not find it easy to convince a stranger.

Determined	Industrious
Motivated Hard working	Easy to get along with
Outgoing/ extraverted	Decisive
Careful	Personal
Shy/ introverted	_____
Timely	_____
Eager to learn	_____
Strong work ethic	_____
Disciplined	_____
Leadership	_____
Tenacious	_____
Responsible	_____

Homework Assignment

Creating Vignettes

Using many of the words in your five rooms noted above; pull out twenty-five vignettes from your history and put them into this format.

V=P+S+B   Vignette =Problem+Solution+Benefit

It is not necessary to write out each one in prose, but it is necessary to give each one a title and say the vignette aloud, pinpointing the problem, solution and benefit. On each of lines below either put a title of your vignette or two words each for P, S or B.

	Problem	Solution	Benefit
1	_____	_____	_____
2	_____	_____	_____
3	_____	_____	_____
4	_____	_____	_____
5	_____	_____	_____
6	_____	_____	_____
7	_____	_____	_____
8	_____	_____	_____
9	_____	_____	_____
10	_____	_____	_____
11	_____	_____	_____
12	_____	_____	_____
13	_____	_____	_____
14	_____	_____	_____
15	_____	_____	_____
16	_____	_____	_____

17 _____ _____ _____
18 _____ _____ _____
19 _____ _____ _____
20 _____ _____ _____
21 _____ _____ _____
22 _____ _____ _____
23 _____ _____ _____
24 _____ _____ _____
25 _____ _____ _____

Homework Assignment

Creating Needs of the Buyer (Bullet Points)

Carefully read the job description five times. If you do not have a job description, find one on the web that is similar or write your own! Find out the duties and responsibilities of the job. Do not include years of experience or educational levels here. Write in bullet point format, the five to seven most important duties and responsibilities of the job being interviewed for.

<u>Duties and Responsibilities</u>

1. _____

2. _____

3. _____

4. _____

5. _____

6. _____

7. _____

Homework Assignment

Matching Benefits with Needs.

Your benefits are your vignettes. You have created 25. Their needs are the 6-8 bullet points created in the last section.

Using 6-8 bullet points as a template, match at least two of your vignettes to each of their needs.

Duties and Responsibilities

1. _____
Recite two vignettes which prove that you can accomplish the above.
 V#_____ V#_____

2. _____
Recite two vignettes which prove that you can accomplish the above.
 V#_____ V#_____

3. _____
Recite two vignettes which prove that you can accomplish the above.
 V#_____ V#_____

4. _____
Recite two vignettes which prove that you can accomplish the above.
 V#_____ V#_____

5. _____
Recite two vignettes which prove that you can accomplish the above.
 V#_____ V#_____

6. _____
Recite two vignettes which prove that you can accomplish the above.
 V#_____ V#_____

7. _____
Recite two vignettes which prove that you can accomplish the above.
 V#_____ V#_____

Homework Assignment

Create an interview plan

From your matching page (previous), where you have coupled your vignettes with their needs, re-list the six or seven vignettes which best match each of the bullet point- needs in the Duties and Responsibilities chart.

Your goal or interview plan is to tell them those six or seven of your best vignettes which match the needs of job description in priority order.

Remember: Each of the interviewer's questions should be converted mentally by you to the question: Can you do the job?

Your answer is always: Yes I can, here is proof.

Your proof is your vignette.

On the previous page you have two vignettes for every need. The extras are your back-ups. Your goal is to be fully prepared.

Interview Plan

1. Vignette#_____.
2. Vignette#_____.
3. Vignette#_____.
4. Vignette#_____.
5. Vignette#_____.
6. Vignette#_____.
7. Vignette#_____.
8. Vignette#_____.

Homework Assignment

The 17 most commonly asked questions on interviews are listed below. One never knows what an interviewer will ask. The key is to be prepared. As a final check on your interviewing skills, ask yourself each of the below listed questions. Convert each one mentally to "Can you do the job?"

See how comfortable you are answering each question with a vignette. The key here is to practice the segue: How do you get from their question to your vignette. Practice makes perfect.

The seventeen questions:

1. Do you understand the position you are applying for?
2. Why are you qualified for this position?
3. What do you bring to the party?
4. What do you put on the plate?
5. What are your strengths? (How would you describe your attributes?)
6. What are your weaknesses?
   Where do you come up short?
   What would you like to improve about yourself?
7. Why are you looking for a job?
8. Why are you interested in this job?
9. How much are you earning?
10. How much do you want to earn?
11. If you could design the ideal situation for yourself, what would it be? Why?
12. What are your immediate goals?

13. Where do you see yourself three years from now? Five years from now?
14. What do you see as your major accomplishments?
15. How have you made a contribution?
16. How would this entity benefit in hiring you?
17. What do you do? What have you done?